BARING-GOULD'S DEVONSHIRE CHARACTERS

Six Devon Rogues

Sabine Baring-Gould

Bossiney Books · Launceston

Contents

First published 2000 by
Bossiney Books, Langore, Launceston, Cornwall PL15 8LD
Based on *Devonshire Characters and Strange Events,* first published 1908
This edition © 2000 Bossiney Books
ISBN 1-899383-33-6
The photograph on the back cover is reproduced by kind permission
of the Royal Institution of Cornwall.
Printed in Great Britain by R Booth (Troutbeck Press), Mabe, Cornwall

Introduction

The short biographies in this book are taken from *Devonshire Characters and Strange Events* by the Rev Sabine Baring-Gould, first published in 1908.

The author (1834-1924) was a most remarkable man. He was for the last forty-three years of his life both squire and parson ('squarson') of Lewtrenchard, a Devon parish lying between Okehampton, Tavistock and Launceston. Much of his childhood had been spent travelling in Europe with his parents, and by the age of fifteen he spoke five languages fluently; this gave him a broad cultural background unusual in an English clergyman of the time, and at the same time he was blessed with a phenomenal energy which allowed him to pursue his many interests.

He became known as a great collector of folk-songs (preceding and then collaborating with Cecil Sharp), as a key player in the study and preservation of the prehistoric remains on Dartmoor, and as a writer of stirring hymns: 'Onward Christian Soldiers' and 'Through the night of doubt and sorrow' are both his. And in between times, he was the architect and site supervisor for building his own new house, supported a huge extended family, and fathered fourteen children – though there is a story that on at least one occasion he asked a little girl, 'Whose child are you my dear?' only to be answered, 'Yours, Daddy.'

He was also a most prolific writer with well over a hundred volumes to his credit on everything from theology to *How to save fuel* and the *History of Sarawak*. His prose, like his personality, is robust and dynamic, and his writing about Devon and Cornwall was immensely popular in his day. His *Lives of the Saints*, in sixteen volumes, produced at six-monthly intervals, was a major compilation of folk-lore rather than traditional hagiography and was consequently included in the Vatican's

Index Expurgatorius as a banned book. He reproduced a great deal of the information in his books from an extraordinarily voluminous memory rather than from checking back with the original source. He had unquenchable self-confidence in his own abilities and judgement in this respect (as indeed in everything he undertook) and can sometimes be faulted in matters of detail.

Although forthright in his opinions, and having certain marked prejudices (for example against Methodists) he was no snob – during his first curacy near Wakefield he had married Grace Taylor, daughter of a mill-hand, and it is said to have been a singularly happy marriage. (She must have been a very tolerant woman!) He also seems to have got on well with the old men from whom, by the pub firesides of Dartmoor, he collected the words and tunes of their traditional music, though whether he understood them or the majority of his parishioners quite as well as he imagined he did is perhaps to be doubted.

What comes over in his writing is that, despite the apparent lack of any self-doubts, he was a man who appreciated the humanity and individuality of people from all walks of life and from every nation, and celebrated their diversity and even their occasional roguery.

The present extracts will hopefully introduce Baring-Gould to a new audience. In *Devon Characters and Strange Events* he made extensive use of printed materials from earlier centuries: we have largely modernised the antiquated spelling and punctuation which he had retained. Some small cuts have also been made, and all the bibliographical references removed for greater accessibility. Since we are dealing with historical documents which are representative of their various periods we have not, for example, changed 'Mohammedanism' to 'Islam'.

Caraboo

On Thursday evening, 3 April, 1817, the overseer of the parish of Almondsbury, in Gloucestershire, called at Knole Park, the residence of Samuel Worall, Esq, to inform him that a young female had entered a cottage in the village, and had made signs to express her desire to sleep there; but not understanding her language, the good folk of the cottage communicated with the overseer, and he, as perplexed as the cottagers, went for counsel to the magistrate. Mr Worall ordered that she should be brought to Knole, and presently the overseer returned with a slim damsel, dressed poorly but quaintly, with a sort of turban about her head, not precisely beautiful, but with very intelligent speaking eyes.

Neither Mr nor Mrs Worall could make heads or tails of what she said. He had a Greek valet who knew or could recognize most of the languages spoken in the Levant, but he also was at fault; he could not catch a single word of her speech that was familiar to him. By signs she was questioned as to whether she had any papers, and she produced from her pocket a bad sixpence and a few halfpence. Under her arm she carried a small bundle containing some necessaries, and a piece of soap wound up in a bit of linen. Her dress consisted of a black stuff gown with a muslin frill round her neck, a black cotton shawl twisted about her head, and a red and black shawl thrown over her shoulders, leather shoes, and black worsted stockings.

The general impression produced from her person and manners was favourable. Her head was small, her eyes black, hair also black; the forehead was low, nose short, in complexion a brunette. The cheeks were faintly tinged with red. The mouth was rather wide, teeth pearly white, lips large and full, the underlip slightly projecting. The chin small and round. Her height was 5ft 2 in. Her hands were clean and small and well cared for. Obviously they had not been accustomed to labour. She wore no ear-rings, but the marks of having worn them remained. Her age appeared to be twenty-five.

After consultation, it was thought advisable to send her to the village inn; and as Mrs Worall was interested in her, she sent her own maid and the footman to attend the stranger to the public-house, it being late in the evening, and to request the landlady to give her a private room and a comfortable bed.

The young woman seemed to be greatly fatigued and walked with difficulty. When shown the room in which she was to sleep, she prepared to lie down on the mat upon the floor; whereupon the landlady put her own little girl into the bed, so as to explain its purport to her guest. The stranger then undressed and went to bed.

Next morning Mrs Worall went to the inn at seven o'clock and found her sitting dejectedly by the fire. The clergyman of the parish had brought some books of travel and illustrated geographies to show her, so that she might give some clue as to whence she came. She manifested pleasure at the pictures of China and the Chinese.

Mrs Worall now took her to Knole, where by signs, pointing to herself and uttering the word Caraboo, she explained to her hostess that this was her name. At dinner she declined all animal food, and took nothing to drink but water, showing marked disgust at beer, cyder, and meat.

Next day she was conveyed to Bristol and examined before the mayor and magistrates, but nothing was made out concerning her, and she was consigned to St Peter's Hospital for Vagrants.

There she remained till the ensuing Monday – three days – refusing food of every description. On that day Mrs Worall went into Bristol and visited her at the hospital. The friendless situation of the foreign lady had in the interim become public, and several gentlemen had called upon her, bringing with them foreigners of their acquaintance, in the hope of discovering who

6

she was. Caraboo expressed lively delight at seeing Mrs Worall again, and that lady, deeply touched, removed her from the hospital to the office of Mr Worall, in Bristol, where she remained for ten days under the care of the housekeeper.

Daily efforts were made to discover her language and country, but without effect. At last a Portuguese of the name of Manuel Eynesso, who happened to be in Bristol, had an interview, and he professed that he was able to interpret what she said. The tale he revealed was that she was a person of consequence in her own country, and had been decoyed from an island in the East Indies, brought to England against her wishes, and then deserted. He further added that her language was not a pure dialect, but was a mixture of several tongues spoken in Sumatra. On this Mrs Worall removed Caraboo to Knole, and from 3 April to 6 June her hostess, the whole family, and the domestics treated her with the utmost consideration and regard.

Among the visitors at Knole was a gentleman who had made many voyages in the East Indies, and he took a lively interest in the girl, and conversed with her, partly by word of mouth and partly – when at fault for words – by signs.

It must have been an interesting sight, the travelled gentleman interrogating Caraboo and taking notes of her reply, with an admiring circle around of the family and visitors, wondering at his linguistic acquirements and facility of speech in Oriental tongues. This traveller committed to writing the following particulars obtained from Caraboo.

She was daughter of a person of high rank, of Chinese origin, by a *Mandin*, or Malay woman, who was killed in war between the Boogoos (cannibals) and the Mandins (Malays). Whilst walking in her garden at Javasu attended by three *sammen* (women), she was seized by pirates commanded by a man named Cheeming, bound hand and foot, her mouth covered, and carried off. She herself in her struggles wounded two of Cheeming's men with her creese; one of these died, the other

7

recovered by the assistance of a *justee* (surgeon). After eleven days she was sold to the captain of a brig called the *Tappa-Boo*. A month later she arrived at a port, presumably Batavia, remained there two days, and then started for England, which was reached in eleven weeks. In consequence of ill usage by the crew, she made her escape to shore. She had had a dress of silk embroidered and interwoven with gold, but she had been induced to exchange this with a woman in a cottage whose doors were painted green, but the situation of which she could not describe.

The garments she now wore were those she had received from the cottager.

After wandering over the country for six weeks, she had arrived at Almondsbury. She spoke of her mother's teeth as artificially blackened (i.e. by chewing betel nut); her face and arms were painted, and she wore a jewel in her nose, and a gold chain from it was attached to her left temple. Her father had three more wives, and he was usually borne upon the shoulders of *macratoos* (common men) in a palanquin.

She described the dress she wore at home. Seven peacock's feathers adorned the right side of her cap or turban. Upon being furnished with calico, she made herself a dress in the style she had been accustomed to. It was short in the skirt, the sleeves wide and long enough to reach to the ground. A broad embroidered band passed round her waist, and the fringe of the skirt, of the sleeves and the bosom, was embroidered. She wore no stockings, and was furnished with sandals of Roman fashion. She sometimes twisted her hair and rolled it up at the top of her head and fastened it with a skewer.

During the ten weeks she resided at Knole and in Bristol, she was never heard to pronounce a word or syllable that at all resembled a European tongue. Mrs Worall's housekeeper, who slept with her, never heard on any occasion any other language, any tone of voice other than those she had employed when she first entered the house.

She was equally constant in her choice of food, and showed great nicety as to her diet. She dressed everything herself, preferring rice to anything else, did not care for bread, rejected meat, and drank only water or tea. She refused a pigeon, which she called a *rampue,* that had been dressed by the cook; but when given a bird that was alive, she pulled off the head, poured the blood into the earth and covered it up, then cooked the bird herself and ate it. This was the only animal food she could be induced to touch, except fish, which she treated in the same manner.

On every Tuesday she fasted rigidly, on which day she contrived to ascend to the roof of the house, frequently at the imminent peril of her life. Ablutions she was particularly fond of; she regularly knelt by the pond in Knole Park and washed her face and hands in it.

After three weeks' residence at Knole, she was one morning missing. But she returned in the evening with a bundle of clothes, her shoes and hands dirty. Then she fell seriously ill.

On Saturday, 6 June, she again took flight. She had not taken with her a pin or needle or ribbon but what had been given to her. She bent her way to Bath, and on the following Sunday, Mrs Worall received information of the place to which her protégée had flown. She determined to reclaim her, and started for Bath, which she reached on Sunday afternoon.

Here she found the Princess of Javasu, as she was called, at the pinnacle of her glory, in the drawing room of a lady of the *haut ton*, one fair lady kneeling at her feet and taking her hand, and another imploring to be allowed the honour of a kiss.

Dr Wilkinson, of Bath, was completely bewildered when he visited her, and wrote to the *Bath Chronicle* a glowing account of Caraboo, in full belief that she was all she pretended to be. "Nothing has yet transpired to authorize the slightest suspicion of Caraboo, nor has such ever been entertained except by those whose souls feel not the spirit of benevolence, and wish to convert into ridicule that amiable disposition in others."

Dr Wilkinson resolved on going to London to consult the Foreign Office, and to obtain funds for the present relief of the Princess, and her restoration to her native land.

Mrs Worall left Bath, taking Caraboo with her. But the wide circulation of the story led to her detection.

On the following Monday, a Mrs Neale called on a Mr Mortimer, and urged him to go to Knole and tell Mrs Worall that she knew the girl very well, for she had lodged in her house in the suburbs of Bristol. At the same time a youth arrived from Westbury, a wheelwright's son, who had met her upon her first expedition to Almondsbury, and remembered seeing her at a public house by the roadside, where a gentleman, feeling compassion for her weariness, had taken her in and treated her to beefsteak and hot rum and water.

Mrs Worall was much disconcerted, but wisely said nothing to her guest of what she had heard, and took Caraboo next day in her carriage to Bristol under the plea that she was going to have Mr Bird, the artist, complete the portrait of the princess on which he was engaged, and desired a final sitting. But instead of driving to Mr Bird's studio, the princess was conveyed to the house of Mr Mortimer, where she was shown into a room by herself, whilst Mrs Worall had an interview with Mrs Neale elsewhere. This lady was attended by her daughter, and their story both surprised and confounded the kind magistrate's wife. After a protracted discussion, she returned to Caraboo, and told her plainly that she was convinced that she was an impostor. When Caraboo heard that Mrs Neale had denounced her, she burst into tears and her fortitude gave way. She made a few feeble attempts to keep up the deception, but finally made a full confession.

Her name was Mary Baker. She was born at Witheridge in Devonshire in 1791, and had received no education, being of a wild disposition and impatient of study. At the age of eight she was employed spinning wool during the winter, and in summer she drove her father's horses, weeded the corn, etc. At the age of sixteen her father and mother procured a situation for her at a farmhouse with a Mr Moon, at Brushford, near Witheridge. She remained there two years as nurse and general help, but left because paid only tenpence a week, and she demanded that her wage should be raised to a shilling, which Mr Moon refused.

Her father and mother were highly incensed at her leaving, and treated her so ill that she ran away from home and went to Exeter, where she knew no one, but had a written character from her former mistress. She was engaged by a shoemaker named Brooke at the wage of £8 per annum. But she remained in this situation only two months. She spent her wage on fine clothes, especially a white gown, and went home in it. Her father was angry at seeing her dressed in white like a lady, and peremptorily ordered her to take the gown off. She refused and left, returned to Exeter, and went about begging. She wandered to Taunton and thence to Bristol, begging from house to house.

From Bristol she made her way to London, where she fell ill with fever, and was taken into St Giles's Hospital. There she enlisted the pity and sympathy of a dissenting preacher, who, when she was well enough to leave, recommended her to a Mrs Matthews, 1 Clapham Road Place, and with her she tarried for three years. Mrs Matthews was very kind to her, and taught her to read; but she was a strict woman, and of the straitest sect of Calvinists. One day Mary heard that there was to be a Jewish wedding in the synagogue near by, and she asked leave to be allowed to witness it. Her mistress refused, but Mary was resolved not to be debarred the spectacle, so she persuaded a servant in a neighbouring house to write a letter to Mrs Matthews, as if from a friend of hers, to say that she was hourly expecting her confinement and was short of domestics: would Mrs Matthews lend her the aid of Mary Baker for a while? Mrs

Matthews could not refuse the favour and sent Mary out of the house, and Mary went to the synagogue and saw what was to be seen there.

Meanwhile, Mrs Matthews had sent to inquire how her dear friend was getting through with her troubles, and expressed a hope that Mary had been of assistance in the house. To her unbounded surprise, she learned that the good lady was not in particular trouble just then, and that she really did not comprehend what Mrs Matthews meant about Mary's assistance. When Mary returned to the house, having seen the breaking of the goblet and heard some psalm singing, she found that a storm was lowering. Her mistress had sent for the dissenting minister to give it hot and strong to the naughty girl. To escape this harangue Mary ran away, wandered about the streets, and seeing a Magdalen Reformatory, applied at the door for admission. "What! so young and so depraved!" was the exclamation with which she was received. She was admitted and remained in the institution some time. Then it was discovered that she had all along not been qualified for admission, and was expelled.

She then exchanged her female garments for a boy's suit at a pawnshop, and started to walk back to Devonshire, begging her way. On Salisbury Plain she fell in with highwaymen, who offered to take her into their company if she could fire a pistol. A pistol was put into her hand, but when she pulled the trigger and it was discharged, she screamed and threw the weapon down. Thereupon the highwaymen turned her off, as a white-livered poltroon unfit for their service. She made her way back to Witheridge to her father, then went into service at Crediton to a tanner, but left her place at the end of three months, unable further to endure the tedium. Then she passed through a succession of services, never staying in any situation longer than three months, and found her way back to London. There, according to her account, she married a foreign gentleman at a Roman Catholic chapel, where the priest officiated to tie the knot. She accompanied her husband to Brighton and thence to Dover, where he gave her the slip, and she had not seen him or heard from him since. She returned to London, was eventually confined, placed her child in the Foundling Institution and then took a situation not far off and visited the child once a week till it died. After a while she again appeared at Witheridge, but her reception was so far from cordial that she left it and associated with gypsies, travelling about with them, telling fortunes.

It was now, according to her account, that the idea entered her head of playing the part of a distinguished stranger from the East, and when she quitted the gypsies, she assumed that part – with what success we have seen.

Mrs Worall sent into Devon to ascertain what amount of truth was in this story. It turned out that her father was named Willcocks, and was a cobbler at Witheridge, and badly off. He confirmed Mary's tale as far as he knew it. She had had an illness when young, and had been odd, restless, and flighty ever since; especially in spring and autumn did she become most impatient and uncontrollable. He denied that he had treated her cruelly, but he had taken the stick to her occasionally, as she was specially aggravating by throwing up every situation obtained for her after staying in it for but a short while.

Finally Mrs Worall got her embarked at Bristol on board a vessel, the *Robert and Anne*, Captain Richardson, under her mother's maiden name of Burgess, for the United States, in the hopes that she might be able to find a situation in Philadelphia.

The reason why she was entered in her mother's name was to prevent her from being overwhelmed by the visits and attentions of the curious. As it was, the Earl of Cork and the Marquess of Salisbury obtained interviews, got the girl to tell her story, speak her lingo, and doubtless did not leave without having put gold into her palm.

She was certainly a remarkable character, with astounding self-possession. Once or twice the housekeeper at Knole would rouse her by some startling cry or call when she was asleep, but even then she never passed out of her assumed character.

At Bath, the lady who had received her into her house proposed that a collection should be made to defray her expenses in returning home to Javasu. Bank-notes were thrown on the table, and some fell off on the floor. Caraboo looked on with stolid indifference. If she picked one up she replaced it on the table without glancing at the note to see how much it was worth; in fact, she acted as if she did not understand that bank-notes were other than valueless scraps of paper.

She was, moreover, insensible to flattery. A young gentleman seated himself by her one day and said, "I think that you are the loveliest creature I ever set eyes on." She remained quite unmoved, not a flutter of colour was in her cheek.

The Greek valet mistrusted her at first, but after a while was completely won over to believe that she was a genuine Oriental princess. She was entirely free from vicious propensities beyond that of feigning to be what she was not. She never purloined anything; never showed any token of wantonness. Vanity and the love of hoaxing people were her prevailing passions; there was nothing worse behind.

So over the blue sea she passed to the West, and what became of her there, whether she gulled the Americans into believing her to be an English countess or marchioness, is unknown.

Of one thing we may be pretty certain, that the gentleman who had visited the Far East, and who pretended to understand her language and thereby drew out her history, never again dared to show his face at Knole.

The authority for this story is: *A narrative of a Singular Imposition practiced by a young woman of the name of Mary Willcocks alias Baker, alias Caraboo, Princess of Javasu*, published by Gutch of Bristol in 1817. This contains two portraits, one by E Bird, RA, the other a full-length sketch of her in her costume as a princess.

Lusty Stucley

If Devonshire has turned out a number, and a very considerable number, of gallant and honourable gentlemen, she has also given birth to some great scoundrels, and one of these was Thomas Stucley or Stukeley. His life was worked out with great pains and elaboration by Richard Simpson in his *School of Shakespeare*, volume 1, 1878.

Captain Thomas Stucley was the third son of Sir Hugh Stucley, of Affeton in the parish of West Worlington, near Chulmleigh. Hugh Stucley, the father of our Thomas was Sheriff of Devon in 1544; his wife was Jane, daughter of Sir Lewis Pollard. Sir Hugh died in 1560.

The eldest son, Lewis Stucley, was aged thirty at the death of his father. He became standard-bearer to Queen Elizabeth.

It was rumoured during the life of Thomas that he was an illegitimate son of Henry VIII, like Sir John Perrot. "Stucley's birth," says Mr Simpson, "must have occurred at the time when the King, tired of his wife Catherine, was as yet ranging among favourites who were contented with something less than a crown as the price of their kindness. Elizabeth Tailbois had been succeeded by Mary Boleyn; and as Mary Boleyn was married to William Carey at Court, and in the presence of the King, 31 January 1521, it is clear that someone else had already succeeded to her place."

Whether Thomas ever claimed to be of royal blood we do not know, but he was certainly treated at foreign courts as one of birth superior to that of a younger son of a Devonshire knight; and the tradition obtains some support from the familiar way in which he was received by both queens, Mary and Elizabeth, and the peculiar terms of intimacy which he assumed towards royal personages.

As a retainer of the Duke of Suffolk, into whose household he had entered, and whose livery he wore, he was present at the siege of Boulogne, 1545-50; and he acted as standard-bearer, with the wage of six shillings and eightpence a day, from 1547 until its surrender to the French in March, 1549-50. Then he returned to England, and attached himself closely to the Protector Somerset.

As one of the Protector's retainers, he was probably involved in his plot to revolutionize the government. The gendarmerie upon the muster day were to be attacked by two thousand men under Sir Ralph Vane, and by a hundred horse of the Duke of Somerset's, besides his friends, who were to stand by, and the idle people who, it was calculated, would take part. After this was done, the Protector intended to run through the city and proclaim, "Liberty! Liberty!" But the plot was discovered in time, and Somerset and his chief accomplices were committed to the Tower, 17 October, 1551. The Council gave orders for Stucley's apprehension, but he escaped in time, and took refuge in France, where he devoted his sword to the service of Henri II, who entitled him "mon cher et bon ami".

He must have fought in the campaign of Henri against the Emperor Charles V in 1552, when Metz was taken by fraud. He was certainly received as a disaffected subject, and was admitted to the French counsels. In 1552 he returned to England with a story which he hoped would purchase his pardon. This was to the effect that Henri II meditated a sudden attack upon Calais.

According to his account the French King himself had spoken to him of the weak points in the defences, had pointed out the very plan of assault by which, six years later, Calais was actually taken. Moreover, according to his scheme, the Scots were to enter Northumberland; Henri II would land troops at Falmouth, and the Duke of Guise would land at Dartmouth, which he knew to be undefended. Cecil suggested that Stucley should be sent back to France to acquire further information; but the Duke of Northumberland sent Stucley's report to the French

King, and committed Stucley to the Tower. Henri denied the truth of what had been reported. The payment of his debts, which had been promised to Stucley as a reward for his revelations, was now refused, and he remained in prison to the end of Edward's reign. He was released on 6 August, 1553, but his debts compelled him again to leave England. Unable to return to France, he betook himself to the Emperor, and he was at Brussels in the winter of 1553-4, and served with the Imperial army at St Omer. Philibert, Duke of Savoy, invited Stucley to accompany him to England in October of 1554, and Stucley accordingly appealed to Queen Mary for security against arrest whilst in her dominions, and this was granted to him for six months, and at the end of December he accompanied the Duke to England.

During his visit he attempted, Othello-like, to bewitch Anne, the grand-daughter and sole heiress of Sir Thomas Curtis, a wealthy alderman of London, with his tales of adventure. Against her father's wishes the lady was beguiled into a secret marriage, and he retired with her to North Devon. On 13 May, 1555, the sheriffs of Devon and Cheshire were ordered to arrest him on a charge of coining false money. His house was searched, his servants questioned. There was much that was suspicious, but nothing certainly to convict. But Thomas Stucley had taken himself off before the sheriff arrived, and again took service under the Duke of Savoy, and shared in the victory of the Imperialists over the French at St Quintin, 10 December, 1557.

Then he went into the Spanish service, but in November old Sir Thomas Curtis died, brokenhearted, it was asserted, at the match his favourite grandchild had contracted with one so disreputable and unprincipled.

Stucley at once returned to England, and a correspondent of Challoner, the Ambassador in Spain, writes of him in November, 1559: "The Alderman Curtis is dead, and by this time is busy Stucley in the midst of his coffers."

Speedily the accumulations of the merchant's industrious life were squandered in extravagance. We next hear of him in April, 1561, when he was appointed to a captaincy in Berwick. There he entertained Shan O'Neil, a famous, turbulent chief from Ireland, who late in this year visited Elizabeth's Court, where his train of kerns and gallowglasses, clothed in linen kilts dyed with saffron, made a great impression.

While at Court, Shan wrote to Elizabeth: "Many of the nobles, magnates, and gentlemen treated me kindly and ingenuously, and, namely, Master Thomas Stucley entertained me with all his heart, and with all the favour he could." The friendship was destined to bear fruit later.

In a few years but little of the alderman's savings remained, and with the wreck that was left, Stucley fitted out a small squadron, and obtained permission from Elizabeth to colonize Florida; and the Queen contributed "2000 weight of corn-powder, and 100 curriers; and besides artillery to the value of £120 towards the furniture of his journey." This was her investment in the venture, though she did not furnish the powder out of her own stores, but made one Bromefield go into debt for it with a Dutchman.

Fuller says that, "having prodigally misspent his patrimony, he entered on several projects (the issue general of all decayed estates), and first pitched on the peopling of Florida, then newly found in the West Indies. So confident his ambition, that he blushed not to tell Queen Elizabeth 'that he preferred rather to be sovereign of a mole-hill than the highest subject to the greatest King in Christendom'; adding, moreover, that 'he was assured he should be a Prince before his death.' 'I hope,' said Queen Elizabeth, 'I shall hear from you, when you are seated in your Principality.' 'I will write to you,' quoth Stucley. 'In what language?' said the Queen. He returned, 'In the style of princes, To our dear Sister.'"

He took leave of the Queen on 25 June, 1563. Cecil wrote in

her name to the Earl of Sussex, Lord Deputy of Ireland: "Our servant Thomas Stucley, associated with sundry of our subjects, hath prepared a number of good ships well armed and manned to pass to discover certain lands to the West towards Florida, and by our licence hath taken the same voyage." But in the event of stormy winds or accidents he was to be well received, should he put into a port in Ireland.

So he sailed, but Stucley had no real intention of going to Florida: his squadron lived by piracy on the high seas for two years. He made his head-quarters at Kinsale, where he resumed acquaintance with Shan O'Neil, chief of Tyrone, who aspired to be king of Ulster, and was repeatedly in arms against the English. Shan had offered Ireland as a fief to Philip II of Spain. And now Stucley from Kinsale swept the seas, and made prizes of Spanish galleons and French and Portuguese merchantmen.

Complaints were made by the foreign courts, and the English Ambassador at Madrid confessed that "he hung his head for shame." Stucley filled his cellars with sherry from Cadiz, and amused Shan O'Neil with his boastful speech, his flattery, and his utterance of what he would do for him; and Shan had the impertinence to write to Elizabeth in favour of "his so dearly loved friend, and her Majesty's worthy subject."

In June, 1563, Stucley took a Zealand ship with £3000 worth of linen and tapestry, and then, joining a small fleet of West-countrymen, fourteen sail in all, he lay off Ushant, watching for the wine fleet from Bordeaux professedly, but picking up gratefully whatever the gods might send. No less a person than the Mayor of Dover himself was the owner of one of these sea-hawks. Wretched Spaniards flying from their talons were dashed to pieces upon the granite cliffs of Finisterre.

At length the remonstrances of foreign ambassadors took effect, and Elizabeth disowned Stucley, and took measures for his apprehension. Some ships were sent out with this object, and he was caught in Cork harbour, in 1565, put under arrest, and sent to London, where he was consigned to the Tower.

Stucley was all the while playing a double game. While professing loyalty to the Queen he was in correspondence with Philip of Spain. Shan O'Neil proposed to Elizabeth that she should divide all Ireland between himself and Stucley, when they would make of it a paradise. Stucley had purchased a good deal of land in Cork, and he hoped to have more granted him and to share with St Leger and Carew in the partition of Munster. He had a plausible tongue, put on an air of great frankness, and soon obtained his release, and was actually sent back to Ireland with a letter of recommendation from Cecil. There he bought of Sir Nicholas Bagnal for £300 down his office of Marshal of Ireland and all Bagnal's estate in the island.

Elizabeth, however, refused to sanction the transaction; she mistrusted him, and with reason, for he was engaged in constant treasonable correspondence with the Spanish Ambassador, and he was in receipt of a pension from Philip. She heard reports of murders, robberies, and other outrages committed by him, and ordered him back to England. He obeyed, cleared himself, and in 1567 was allowed to return to Ireland, where he purchased of Sir Nicholas Heron the offices of seneschal and constable of Wexford and captainship of the Kavanaghs, together with many estates. Again Elizabeth interfered, and Stucley was turned out of his offices. Nicholas White, Heron's successor, now accused Stucley of felony and high treason, and in June, 1569, he was imprisoned in Dublin Castle. It was high time; he had in that same month proposed to Philip the invasion of Ireland, and had demanded twenty fully armed ships for the purpose. As sufficient evidence to convict him was not forthcoming, he was discharged, but felt that he could no longer rely on Elizabeth's forbearance. With treachery in his heart he pretended to Sidney, the Queen's deputy in Ireland, that after such misinterpretation of his acts and doubts of his fidelity, he desired to go in person to his royal mistress and clear his reputation with her; and

Sidney, instead of sending him over under a guard, was contented with his parole – Stucley's parole!

Stucley informed him that for his defence he needed a certain number of Irish gentlemen to serve as witnesses to his conduct. The deputy permitted him to purchase and fit out a ship at Waterford to transport them and himself. He took with him some Irish cavaliers, along with their servants and horses, and a miscellaneous crew of adventurers. They embarked as for London, but when clear of the harbour made for the ocean. A few days after they sailed for Galicia, and sent messengers to Philip to announce their arrival.

The Archbishop of Cashel, then at Madrid, not knowing much of Stucley, recommended Philip to receive the party. The King accordingly sent for him to Court, knighted him, loaded him with presents, granted him five hundred reales a day and a residence, at Las Rozas, nine miles from Madrid, where he lived in great state, with thirty gentlemen about him. He made great brag of the vast estates of which the Queen had deprived him – Wexford, Kinsale, the Kavanagh country, Carlow, and the whole kingdom of Leinster, and an income of £2200 per diem – and was believed. He assumed the title of Duke of Ireland, but Philip only allowed him to be received as Duke of Leinster. He represented himself as of vast influence in Ireland, and Philip was completely taken in by his boasting. But the Archbishop of Cashel soon received tidings of his real position in the island. He had robbed churches, despoiled abbeys, was detested by the native Irish whom he had cruelly maltreated, and was of no influence at all.

Thenceforth two parties were formed in the Spanish Court, one denouncing Stucley as an adventurer and so unprincipled that if he thought it would suit his purpose he would betray everything to Elizabeth. The other party believed in his professions and encouraged the King to trust him; and his assumption, his audacious and enormous lies, his perfect self-assurance bore down all opposition, and under Stucley's auspices the Spanish Government began serious preparations for the invasion and conquest of Ireland. Ships were collected at Vigo with arms and stores. Ten thousand men were to be raised, and Julian Romero was to be recalled from Flanders to command.

Meanwhile he amused the Spaniards with scandalous stories about Elizabeth and her Court, and his fool's boast of what he was about to achieve.

"Master Stucley said to the King's Council that the Queen's Majesty will beat Secretary Cecil about the ears when he discontenteth her, and he will weep like a child. The Spaniards asking him why the Queen's Highness did not marry, he said she would never marry, for she cannot abide a woman with child, for she saith those women be worse than a sow. He also said, 'What hurt I can do her I will do it and will make her vilely afraid.'"

"The Duke's Grace Stucley had received the Sacrament, and promised to render unto the King of Spain not only entrance within his duchy, but also possession of the whole realm of Ireland. The soldiers were amassing from all parts of Spain – Spaniards, Burgundians, Italians, the most part Bezonians, beggarly, ill-armed rascals, but their captains old beaten men-of-war. The King was sparing no cost on the enterprise, and no honours to Stucley, hoping by such means to enlarge his empire."

Nothing, however, came of this at the time, and the party that perceived Stucley to be a charlatan grew stronger, his boasting palled, and the King at last became suspicious and withdrew his favour. Perceiving himself to be regarded on all sides with mistrust, not to say with contempt, in a huff he left Spain, went to Italy, and offered his service to the Pope. In 1571 he was given command of three galleys, and partook in Don John's victory over the Turks at Lepanto; and thus raised himself considerably in King Philip's estimation. Then he went back to Rome, where "it is incredible how quickly he wrought himself into the favour, through the Court into the chamber, yea closet, yea bosom of Pope Pius V; so that some wise men thought his Holiness did forfeit a parcel of his Infallibility in giving credit to such a *glorioso,* vaunting that with three thousand soldiers, he would beat all the English out of Ireland."

The Pope created Stucley Baron of Ross, Viscount Murrough, Earl of Wexford, and Marquess of Leinster, and furnished him with a few vessels and eight hundred soldiers, but these were to receive their pay from the King of Spain.

Some contention arose as to the division of spoil when Elizabeth was overthrown and England and Ireland were at the feet of Gregory XIII and Philip of Spain. The Pope gave Stucley a consecrated banner to plant in Ireland, which was to become wholly his own, and to which he was to appoint the Pope's bastard son, Giacomo Buoncompagni, as king.

Stucley left Civita Vecchia in March, 1578, but soon found that the vessels were unseaworthy, and the military the off-scouring of Italy. Stucley put into Lisbon for repairs, and found King Sebastian of Portugal preparing for his attempt on North Africa, having with him two Moorish kings. The King persuaded Stucley to accompany him. Landing in Africa, Stucley gave wise counsel to Sebastian not to engage the enemy till the soldiers had recovered from the voyage, they having suffered severely in the stormy passage. But the young King would listen to no advice, and in the battle of Alcazar, on 4 August, 1578, Stucley lost his life, regretted probably by none.

Thus perished a man of whom Cecil had written some years before, "Thomas Stucley, a defamed person almost through all Christendom, and a faithless beast rather than a man, fleeing first out of England for notable piracies, and out of Ireland for treacheries unpardonable."

Lord Burghley also wrote: "Of this man might be written whole volumes to paint out the life of a man in the highest degree of vain-glory, prodigality, falsehood, and vile and filthy conversation of life, and altogether without faith, conscience, or religion."

Stucley at once became the hero of ballads, chapbooks, and plays. *The Famous History of the Life and Death of Captain Thomas Stukeley* was printed in 1605, and Peele's *Battle of Alcazar* in 1594, but both plays had been acted before these dates. In the *Life and Death* Stucley is glorified, as an idol of the military or Essex party to which Shakespeare is known to have belonged, and it has been thought that his hand can be traced in the composition. But if so, he has left in it but little trace of his genius.

In one of the ballads published about Stucley, he is thus spoken of:

> Taverns and ordinaries
> Were his chiefest braveries,
> Golden angels there flew up and down;
> Riots were his best delights
> With stately feasting day and night,
> In court and city thus he won renown.

Joanna Southcott

The life of this impostor or self-deluded woman is not pleasant to write or to read, and it is only because in such a collection including Devonshire oddities and unworthies she could not be excluded that her story is here given.

Joanna was a native of Gittisham, the daughter of William and Hannah Southcott, respectable people, the father a very small farmer. She was baptized at Ottery St Mary, on 6 June 1750. There was nothing remarkable in her during the first forty years of her life. She was in domestic service, and then moved to Exeter, where she entered the household of an upholsterer, in 1790.

What turned her head was the visit of a revivalist Methodist preacher, who, combining the most fiery evangelic preaching with laxity of morals, lived in adultery with her mistress, and endeavoured to seduce the daughter. But his ministrations in the pulpit were acceptable. He shrieked and threatened till sometimes the whole congregation fell flat and rigid on the floor, when he would walk in and out among them and revive them by assuring them they had received pardon for all their sins, were elect vessels, and that their election was sealed in heaven. He would declare that there never was a man so highly favoured of God as himself, and that he would not thank God to make him other than what he was, unless he made him greater than every other man on earth, and placed supreme power in his hands; and he boasted, when he heard of the death of a man who had derided his mission, that he had prayed this man to death.

All the servants in the house were afraid of this preacher; but Joanna affirmed that he had no power over her, and that she was wont to think that the room was full of spirits when he was engaged in prayer. But though she fancied this man had no power over her, he certainly had, and turned her into a fanatic, intoxicating her with his own spiritual pride.

When first she went to Exeter, she attended the services in the cathedral, but she left the Church and joined the Wesleyans in 1791, as she affirmed, by Divine command, for she was already beginning to see visions. The ministers of the sect frequented her master's shop, and took a good deal of notice of Joanna, and this encouraged her to launch forth in the course she afterwards pursued. In 1792 she stated that she had had a vision of the Lord, and a meeting of Methodist preachers was summoned to discuss her spiritual condition. It concluded by their signing a paper to the effect that her calling was of God.

One of the Methodist preachers in Exeter was named Pomeroy, and he at first more than half believed in her mission. She gave him a number of sealed packets, which she told him contained her prophecies, and desired him to keep them till a time she mentioned, when they were to be opened and would prove the truth of her claim to inspiration.

The minister received the precious papers; but afterwards, when Joanna publicly announced that he was a believer and a recipient of her prophecies, he got frightened, and committed the unopened predictions to the flames. "From that time," says Southey [in *Letters from England*], "all the Joannians, who are now a considerable number, regard him as the arch-apostate. He is the Jehoiakim, who burnt Jeremiah's roll; he is their Judas Iscariot, a second Lucifer. They call upon him to produce those prophecies, which she boldly asserts, and they implicitly believe, have all been fulfilled, and therefore would convince the world of the truth of her mission. In vain does Mr Pomeroy answer that he has burnt these unhappy papers: in an unhappy hour for himself did he burn them! Day after day long letters are dispatched to him, sometimes from Joanna herself, sometimes from her brother, sometimes from one of her four-and-twenty elders, filled with exhortation, invective, texts of Scripture, and denunciations of the law in this world and the devil in the next; and these letters the prophetess prints, for the very sufficient reason – that all her believers purchase them. Mr Pomeroy sometimes treats them with contempt; at other times he appeals to their compassion, and beseeches them, if they have any bowels of Christian charity, to have compassion on him and let him rest."

Meanwhile, the falling away of this believer was abundantly compensated to Joanna by the accession of other adherents, both lay and clerical. Among the persons of superior station in the world who became ardent disciples was the Rev T P Foley, incumbent of Old Swinford, in Leicestershire, who should have written his name Folly, not Foley.

In 1792 she had a serious illness, and went to Plymtree to recruit [recuperate]. When she was recovered she set to work again with renewed vigour. She pretended to have found, whilst sweeping the house, a die with "J.S." on it between two stars, and this she used henceforth for sealing her prophecies and her passports to heaven.

But she had other disappointments, beside the defection of Mr Pomeroy. One of the elders, Elias Carpenter, of Bermondsey, after going a certain way with her, fell off. This, however, was later. He was followed by six others. Thereupon she wrote and printed five letters of denunciation and woe to the backsliders.

By the sale of her sealed passports to heaven Joanna obtained a very respectable revenue, and from being a poor working drudge she blossomed out into a woman of substance. Her followers in Exeter were recognized by the peculiarity of their dress, somewhat in the fashion of that of the Quakers, the men being particularly distinguished by wearing a long beard at a time when beards were not generally adopted.

In 1798 she moved to Bristol, and in 1801 began to publish books of prophecies and warnings, which were eagerly purchased by her followers. In 1802 she moved to London, where she was patronized by Sharp, the engraver, and had other influential friends, Brothers, the fanatic, who had proclaimed himself the promised Messiah, and a certain Miss Cott, whom he admitted to be the daughter of King David and the future Queen of the Hebrews. But Richard Brothers was sent to Bridewell, and those who had believed in him, amongst others an MP, Mr Halhead, member for Lymington, were drifting about in quest of some new delusion. Joanna suited them to a nicety, and they rallied about her.

The books which she sent forth into the world were written partly in prose, partly in rhyme, all the prose and most of the rhyme being given forth as the direct words of the Almighty. It is not possible to conceive that any persons could have been deluded by such rambling nonsense, did one not know that human folly is like the Well of Zemzem that is inexhaustible.

Joanna's handwriting was illegibly bad; so that at last she found it advisable to pretend that she had received orders from heaven to discard the pen, and deliver her oracles verbally, and the words flowed from her faster than the scribes could write them down. Her prophecies were words, and words only, a rhapsody of texts and vulgar applications; the verse the vilest doggerel ever written, and the rhyme and grammar equally bad. She made a pretty penny, not only by the sale of her books, but also by her "Certificates for the Millennium" and her "Sealings of the Faithful", passports to paradise. Of these she sold between six and seven thousand, some at twelve shillings, but most at a guinea; and she continued the sale until a woman, Mary Bateman, a Leeds murderess, who had poisoned a Mrs Perigo, and had attempted to poison Mr Perigo, was hanged in 1809, and it was ascertained that this poisoner had been furnished by Joanna with one of her passports to paradise.

In 1813, she first announced that she was to become the mother of Shiloh, that she was the Woman spoken of in the Apocalypse as having the moon under her feet, and on her head a crown of twelve stars; the twelve stars were twelve evangelists or apostles whom she sent abroad to declare her revelations. In herself, she asserted, the scheme of redemption would be completed: by woman came the fall of man, and by woman must come his restoration. She was the Bride, the promised seed who was to bruise the serpent's head. The evening-star was placed in the firmament to be her type. The immediate object of her call was to destroy the devil; of this Satan was fully aware; and that it might not be said he had foul play, a regular dispute of seven days was agreed upon between him and Joanna, in which she was to be alone; the conditions were that if she held out her argument for seven days, Satan should retire from troubling the earth, but if she yielded, then his kingdom was to stand. Accordingly, she went alone into a solitary house for this contest. Joanna on this occasion was her own secretary, and the *procès verbal* of the conference was printed from her manuscript. She set down all Satan's blasphemies with the utmost frankness, and the proficiency he displayed in vulgar language and Billingsgate abuse is surprising.

Of all Joanna's books this is the most curious. The conference terminated like most theological disputes. Both parties grew warm; but Joanna's tongue was more lightly slung on its pivots, and she talked Satan out of all patience. She gave him, as he complained, ten words to his one, and allowed him no time to speak. All men, he said, were already tired of her tongue, and now she had tired the devil.

This was not unreasonable; but he proceeded to abuse the whole sex, which would be ungracious in any one, but in him was peculiarly ungrateful. He said that no man could tame a woman's tongue; it were better to dispute with a thousand men than with one woman.

Once she declared that she had scratched the devil's face with her nails, and had even bitten off one of his fingers, and that his blood tasted sweet.

When she announced to the world her pregnancy, her followers were filled with breathless expectation. Presents came pouring in for the coming Shiloh. One wealthy proselyte sent a cradle that cost £200, manufactured by Seddons, a cabinet-maker of repute in Aldersgate Street; another sent a pap-spoon that cost £100; and that nothing might be lacking at this accouchement laced caps, infant's napkins, bibs, mantles, some of white satin, pap-boats, caudle-cups arrived. A Bible also, richly bound, was not forgotten as a present to the coming Messiah. The cradle is now in Salford Museum.

But what was most extraordinary of all is that a regular London physician, a Dr Richard Reece, having on 7 August, 1814, visited Joanna, "to ascertain the probability of her being in a state of pregnancy, as then given out," declared his opinion to be that she was perfectly right in the view she had taken of her situation, and according to his own admission in a four-shilling pamphlet, entitled *A Correct Statement of the Circumstances, etc.*, which he published, declared his belief in the fact.

No wonder that after this the Rev Mr Foley, who had headed a deputation that waited on the doctor to obtain an authentic declaration, and the whole body of the believers, were frantic with exultation and confidence; and that even a portion of the hitherto incredulous public began to have misgivings, and not to know very well what to think of the matter.

When Dr Reece first saw the prophetess she expected to lie-in in a few weeks; months however passed without bringing the looked-for event. Further, to strengthen the delusion, it was unblushingly asserted that a number of medical men of the highest reputation had been called in, and that they had expressed their opinion affirmatively as to her pregnancy.

Dr Sims, however, published a statement to this effect in the *Morning Chronicle* of 3 September, 1814: "I went to see her on August 18th, and after examining her, I do not hesitate to declare, it is my firm opinion, that the woman called Joanna

Southcott is not pregnant; and, before I conclude this statement, I feel it right to say, that I am convinced the poor woman labours under strong mental delusion."

A Mr Want, also a surgeon, who was called in by Dr Reece, unhesitatingly declared his opinion that she was not in the family way, as also that there were no hopes of her recovery.

Before her death, which took place on 27 December, she had been confined to her bed for above ten weeks. During this time she had lived in a state of mental exaltation, but towards the end her courage failed. A scene in the chamber of the dying woman, which Dr Reece relates that he witnessed on 19 November, is not without pathos.

Five or six of the believers, who had been waiting, having been admitted, "She desired them to be seated round her bed; when, spending a few minutes in adjusting the bed-clothes with seeming attention, and placing before her a white handkerchief, she thus addressed them, as nearly as I can recollect, in the following words: 'My friends, some of you have known me nearly twenty-five years, and all of you not less than twenty. When you have heard me speak of my prophecies, you have sometimes heard me say that I doubted my inspiration. But, at the same time, you would never let me despair. When I have been alone it has often appeared delusion; but when the communications were made to me I did not in the least doubt. Feeling, as I now do feel, that my dissolution is drawing near, and that a day or two may terminate my life, it all appears a delusion.' She was by this exertion quite exhausted, and wept bitterly."

She then, the doctor proceeds to inform us, after some further discourse about her death and funeral, wept again, and some of those present also shed tears; but after a little while, one of them, Mr Howe, spoke up, and said: "Mother, your feelings are human. We know you are a favoured woman of God, and that you will produce the promised child, and whatever you may say to the contrary will not diminish our faith."

This assurance, we are told, revived her, and from crying she fell to laughing. She however then made her will.

Immediately on her decease, Dr Reece wrote to the editor of the *Sunday Monitor*, which had lent itself to become an organ of the Joannites:

"Agreeably to your request, I send a messenger to acquaint you, that Joanna Southcott died this morning, precisely at 4 am. The believers in her mission, supposing that the vital functions are only suspended for a few days, will not permit me to open the body until some symptom appears, which may destroy all hopes of resuscitation."

In fact, in 1792, Joanna had published a prophecy to the effect that she, the mother of Shiloh, previous to his birth would be as dead for four days, and at the end of that period would revive and be delivered. No sooner was she dead than her friends proceeded to wrap her body in warm blankets, to place bottles of hot water at her feet, and by keeping the room warm, to endeavour to preserve the vital spark.

Manchester Street was thronged by a crowd watching the house, and inquiries respecting her resuscitation were constant and anxious. To all inquiries the answer given was consolatory. On Saturday the crowd again assembled early, before 4 am, and the most zealous pronounced their positive conviction that she would come to life again that day.

But the prescribed period of four days and nights elapsed, and so far was the body from exhibiting appearances of a temporary suspension of animation, that it began to display a discoloration which at once brought home to conviction the fact that the wretched Joanna was but mortal. Preparations were made to dissect her remains. A summons was issued to the surgeons who had expressed a wish to be present, and at 2 pm fifteen gentlemen assembled; in addition were the apostle Tozer, Colonel Harwood, and one or two other of Joanna's followers and proselytes. Ann Underwood was in the ante-room, much chagrined at the disappointment of her hopes, and the breakdown of her convictions.

The examination of the body showed that Joanna Southcott had been suffering from dropsy, which had killed her.

The adherents of the prophetess, who had awaited the event, skulked off in great tribulation, and were happy to escape the populace, who were outrageous towards any whom they suspected of adhering to the sect of Joanna. This excusable indignation had nearly proved fatal in the morning to an old lady who had rapped at the door of the house, to make inquiries as to whether Joanna was already resuscitated. No sooner was she suspected to be a disciple, than she was assailed with mud and cabbage stalks.

Some glimmerings of sanity had lightened the mind of Joanna previous to her death, and she had indited a will, in which she professed that she had been a deceiver, prompted to play her part by the devil, and directing that after her death, cradle, caudlecups, pap-boats, etc, that had been sent for the use of the coming Shiloh, should be returned to the donors. She was buried in Marylebone burying-ground on 2 January, 1815. On her stone was inscribed:

In Memory of Joanna Southcott,
who departed this life December 27, 1814, aged 60 years.

While through all my wondrous days,
Heaven and earth enraptured gaze,
While vain sages think they know
Secrets thou alone canst show,
Time alone will tell what hour
Thou'lt appear in greater power!

The composition evidently of one of her dupes, hoping on still. She was really aged sixty-four years. Her tombstone was shattered by the great gunpowder explosion in the Regent's Park Canal in 1874. The delusion was not at an end with the death and burial of Joanna. Sharp, the engraver, ever after maintained that she was not really dead, and would rise again and become the mother of Shiloh. When he was sitting to Haydon for his portrait, he predicted that Joanna would reappear in the month of July, 1822.

"But suppose she should not?" said Haydon.

"I tell you that she will," retorted Sharp, "but if she should not, nothing would shake my faith in her divine mission."

Those who were near Sharp during his last illness, state that in this belief he died.

Nor was he singular. Some of her one hundred thousand adherents fell away, but a great many remained, waiting in yearly expectation for her reappearance. The men bound themselves by a vow not to shave their beards till her resurrection. It need scarcely be said that they descended to their graves unshorn.

Under the date of January, 1817, the *Annual Register* quotes the following notice of the proceedings of the sect from a Lincoln newspaper of the day: "An interdict arrived at Newark, on Sunday, the 19th instant, from a disciple of the Conclave at Leeds, inhibiting those of the faith, amongst other things, from attending to their ordinary business during the ensuing eight or nine days; and a manufacturer's shop at that place is at this time entirely deserted, and the business of many small dealers suspended in consequence." This was due to the expectation of the resuscitation of Joanna.

Leeds was one of the strongholds of Joannism, and several of the founder's publications are dated from that place.

In January, 1817, some two years after her death, the London disciples made a remarkable outbreak. One morning, having assembled somewhere in the West End of the metropolis, they made their way to Temple Bar, passing through which, they set forward in procession through the City, each decorated with a white cockade, and wearing a small star of yellow riband on the left breast. In this guise, led by one of their number, carrying a brazen trumpet ornamented with light blue ribands, while two boys marching by his side bore each a flag of silk, they proceeded along Fleet Street, up Ludgate Hill, and thence through St Paul's Churchyard to Bridge Row, followed by the rabble in great force.

Here, having reached what they considered to be the centre of the great city, they halted; and then their leader sounded his trumpet, and roared out that the Shiloh, the Prince of Peace, was come again to the earth; to which a woman who was with him, and who was said to be his wife, responded with another wild cry of "Woe! woe! to the inhabitants of the earth, because of the coming of Shiloh."

This terrific vociferation was repeated several times, and joined in by the rest of the party. But at last the mob, which now completely blocked up the street, from laughing and shouting proceeded to pelting the enthusiasts with mud and harder missiles. They struggled to make their escape, or to beat off their assailants; this led to a general fight; the flags were torn, and the affray ended in the trumpeter and his wife, five other men and the two boys of the party, after having been rolled in the mire, being rescued from the fury of the multitude by the constables, and conveyed to the Compter [a prison].

When they were brought up the next day before the alderman at Guildhall, they maintained that they were only obeying the commands of God in acting as they had done. Their spokesman, the trumpeter, who turned out to be one Sibley, a City watchman, who appeared to exercise great authority over the others, said that he had proclaimed the second coming of the Shiloh in the same manner and with the same authority as John the Baptist, who had announced the first coming; and his wife asserted that she had had the Shiloh in her arms four times. In the end they were all sent back to prison, to be detained till they could find security for their peaceful demeanour in future.

A remnant of the sect, the Jezreelites, lingered on for long at

Chatham, remarkable for the general singularity of their manners and appearance.

The Joannites are now almost, if not wholly, extinct, leaving room for some newer outbreak of religious folly.

If we did not live at a period when such charlatans as Dr Dowie and Mrs Eddy have appeared, drawn about them crowds of adherents, and conjured tens of thousands of pounds out of their pockets, we should have supposed that such irruptions of religious mania, such eagerness to believe in a lie, such credulous clinging to an impostor, were a thing of the remote past. But the fools, like the poor, are always with us, and

Still Dunce the Second reigns like Dunce the First.

The question presents itself to the mind whether Joanna was a conscious impostor, or whether she was self-deluded. With her dying confession and her will before us, it would seem that she knew that she was imposing on the credulity of men and women. She had seen a debauched and dissolute Methodist preacher in her master's house pose as an apostle and as inspired, and draw crowds and convince them that he was an oracle of God. She imitated him, and found that her imitation was successful, and also that it paid well. She was able to command thousands of pounds from her dupes, and it flattered her vanity to be appreciated as one half divine.

She had occasional qualms of conscience, but her devotees had more faith in her than she had in herself, and they overbore every feeble attempt to retrace her steps.

Sir John Fitz

Tavistock, in the reign of Elizabeth, was a more picturesque town than it is at present.

Then the abbey walls, crenellated and with towers at intervals, were still standing in complete circuit, and the abbey church, the second finest in the county and diocese, though unroofed, was still erect. The houses, slate-hung in quaint patterns representing fleurs-de-lis, oak leaves, swallow-tails, pomegranates, with gables to the street, were very different from the present houses, stuccoed drab and destitute of taste. Moreover the absurd, gaunt market hall erected last century was not a central and conspicuous disfigurement to the town.

But a few strides to the west, on the Plymouth road, stood Fitzford House, a mansion recently erected, consisting of a court, entered through a massive gatehouse, and the mansion standing back, with porch and projecting wings.

In this house lived the Fitz family. They had been there for four generations and had married well. They were also well estated, with property in Cornwall, in Kent and Southwark, as well as in Devon. John Fitz, the father of the man whose tragic history we are about to relate, married Mary, daughter of Sir John Sydenham, of Brimpton, in Somerset, and had late in life one son, the "unfortunate" Sir John. The Fitzes had been a family bred to the law; the first known of them, John Fitz, had been a bencher of Lincoln's Inn, and the John Fitz who married Mary Sydenham was also a counsellor-at-law, and he managed considerably to add to the wealth of the family. When he had got as much as he wanted out of the pockets of his clients, he retired to his family place of Fitzford and there amused himself with astrology and the casting of horoscopes. When his son John was about to be born in 1575, John Fitz studied the stars, and, says Prince [*Worthies of Devon*, 1701], "finding at that time a very unlucky position of the heavens, he desired the midwife, if possible, to hinder the birth but for one hour; which, not being to be done, he declared that the child would come to an unhappy end and undo the family."

John Fitz the elder was riding over the moor one day with his wife, when they lost their direction, were, in fact, pixy-led, and they floundered through bogs, and could nowhere hit on the packhorse track that led across the moors from Moreton Hampstead to Tavistock. Exhausted and parched with thirst they lighted on a crystal stream, dismounted, and drank copiously of the water. Not only were they refreshed, but at once John Fitz's eyes were opened, the spell on him was undone, and he knew where he was and which direction he should take. Thereupon he raised his hand and vowed he would honour that well, so that such travellers as were pixy-led might drink at it and dispel the power over them exercised by the pixies.

The spring still flows and rises under a granite structure erected in fulfilment of his vow by John Fitz; it bears his initials and the date 1568 in raised figures and letters on the covering stone. Formerly it was on a slope in the midst of moorland away from the main track, near the Blackabrook. Now it is enclosed in the reclaimed tract made into meadows by the convicts of Princetown. Happily the structure has not been destroyed: it is surrounded by a protecting wall.

In the same year that John Fitz erected this well, he obtained a lease to carry water in pipes of wood or of lead through the garden of one John Northcott to his mansion at Fitzford. The little house that he built over the spring in his close, called Boughthayes, still stands, picturesquely wreathed in ivy.

He died 8 January, 1589-90, aged sixty-one, and by his will made his wife executrix and guardian of his son, who was then rather over fourteen years old. There is a stately monument in Tavistock Parish Church to John Fitz and his wife, he clothed in armour which in life he probably never wore, as he was a man of the long robe. The effigies are recumbent, and by them is a smaller, kneeling figure of the son and heir, their only child, the "unfortunate" John Fitz. But the widow did not have charge of her son; as a ward under the Queen he was committed to Sir Arthur Gorges, "who tended more to the good of the child than his own private profit", which was perhaps unusual. Mary Fitz retired to Walreddon, near Tavistock, another house belonging to the family, for her initials M.F. and the date 1591 are cut in granite over the doorway. But presently she married Christopher Harris, of Radford, when she moved to his house near Plymouth.

The young John Fitz was described as "a very comely person". He was married, before he had attained his majority, to Bridget, sixth daughter of Sir William Courtenay. Of this marriage one child, Mary, was born 1 August, 1596, when her father was just twenty-one years old. John Fitz was now of age, considered himself free of all restraint, owner of large estates, was without stability of character or any principle, and was inclined to a wild life. He took up his residence at Fitzford, and roistered and racketed at his will.

One day (it was 4 June, 1599) he was dining at Tavistock with some of his friends and neighbours. The hour was early, for in the account of it we are told that "with great variety of merriments and discourse they outstripped the noontime."

John Fitz had drunk a good deal of wine, and he began to brag of his possessions, and boasted that he had not a foot of land that was not his freehold. Among those present was Nicholas Slanning, of Bickleigh. He interrupted Fitz, and said, "That is not so. You hold of me a parcel of land that is copyhold, and though of courtesy it has been intermitted, yet of due, you owe me so much a year for that land."

John started from his seat, and told Slanning to his face that he lied, and mad with rage, drew his dagger and would have stabbed him. Slanning with a knife beat down Fitz's blade, and the friends at the table threw themselves between them and patched up the quarrel as they supposed. Nicholas Slanning then left the apartment and departed for Bickleigh with his man, both being on horseback.

They had not ridden far when they came to a deep and rough descent, whereupon Slanning bade his man lead the horses, and, dismounting, walked through a field where the way was easier.

At that moment he saw John Fitz with four attendants galloping along the lane after him. Without ado, Slanning awaited the party and inquired of John Fitz what he desired of him. Fitz replied that he had followed that he might avenge the insult offered him. Thereupon Fitz called to his men, and they drew their blades and fell on Slanning, who had to defend himself against five men. The matter might even then have been composed, but one of Fitz's men, named Cross, twitted his master, saying, "What play is this? It is child's play. Come, fight!" Fitz, who had sheathed his sword, drew it again and attacked Slanning. The latter had long spurs, and stepping back they caught in a tuft of grass, and as he staggered backward, Fitz ran him through the body. At the same time, one of Fitz's men struck him from behind. Slanning fell to the ground and died. He was conveyed home, and buried in Bickleigh Church, where his monument still exists, but in a mutilated condition. It was of plaster, and when the church was "restored" fell to pieces; but the curious Latin inscription has been preserved.

Nicholas Slanning had been married to Margaret, daughter of Henry Champernowne, of Modbury, and he died leaving as his heir a child; the administration of his estates was committed to that son's great-uncle. Of Ley, the fine Slanning place, nothing now remains except the balls that stood on the entrance gates, that have been transferred to the vicarage garden at Bickleigh. The situation was incomparably beautiful, and it is to be regretted that the grand old Elizabethan mansion has been levelled with the dust. Sir Nicholas Slanning, created a baronet in 1663, moved to Maristowe in Tamerton Foliot, but the second and last baronet died without issue in 1700.

"Great," we are informed, "was the lamentation that the countryside made for the death of so beloved a gentleman as Maister Slanning was."

John Fitz, then aged twenty-four, escaped to the Continent and stayed in France, until the exertions of his wife and mother succeeded in December, 1599, in procuring a pardon for him; whereupon he returned home, unsubdued by the past, insolent, riotous, and haughty. At the coronation of James I, 1603, he was knighted, not for services done to the Crown or State, but because he was of good family, well connected, and with property.

He returned to Fitzford, where, finding his wife and child something of a drag upon him in his wild and dissipated career, he turned them out of doors, and his wife had to go for shelter to her father. Left now to himself and his evil associates, "men of dissolute and desperate fortunes", chief among whom was "Lusty Jack, one whose deeds were indeed mean, whose qualities altogether none," he behaved in such sort that "the town of Tavistock, though otherwise orderly governed with sobriety, and likewise of grave magistrates, was thereby infected with the beastly corruption of drunkenness. Sir John, of his own inclination apt, and by his retained copesmates urged, persevered evermore to run headlong into such enormities as their sensuality and pleasures inclined unto, spending their time in riotous surfeiting and in all abominable drunkenness, plucking men by night out of their beds, violently breaking windows, quarrelling with ale-conners [beer-tasters], fighting in private brables amongst themselves. And when they had abused the townsmen and disturbed their neighbours, Sir John's own house was their sanctuary or receptacle to cloak their outrages; so as it seemed they lived as, in time of old, the common outlaws of the land did, neither worshipping God nor honouring Prince, but wholly subject to their contents alone."

According to Prince, about this time Fitz committed another murder; but what seems to be better authenticated is that he all but killed one of the town constables.

In the summer of 1605, Sir John Fitz was summoned to London to appear before the courts, in answer to a claim of compensation for their father's murder, made by the children of Nicholas Slanning, the eldest of whom, Gamaliel, was now about eighteen years old. He set out on horseback, attended by a servant. Dissipation had weakened his mind and shattered his nerves. He was in deadly alarm. Not only would he be heavily fined for the assassination of Slanning, but he had been playing ducks and drakes with his property which had been settled by deed of 20 March, 1599, on his wife, and he expected to be called to task for this by Sir William Courtenay, his wife's father.

He took it into his head that his life was in danger, that the friends and kinsfolk of Slanning would ambuscade and murder him; that Sir William Courtenay would be willing to have him put out of the way so as to save the property from being further dissipated. At every point on his journey he showed himself suspicious of being waylaid or pursued. Every day his fancies became more disordered.

At length he reached Kingston-upon-Thames, and put up for the night there. But he could not sleep, noises disturbed him, and rising from his bed he insisted on the servant getting ready his nag, and away he rode over Kingston Bridge, alone, having peremptorily forbidden his man to accompany him, entertaining some suspicion that the man had been bought by his enemies and would lead him into a trap. He drew up at the "Anchor", a small tavern at Twickenham kept by one Daniel Alley; it was now 2 am, and all Twickenham was asleep. He hammered at the door and shouted; presently the casement opened, and the publican put out his head and inquired what the gentleman wanted. Sir John demanded a bed and shelter for the rest of the night. Daniel Alley begged to be excused, he had no spare room, his house was small and not fitted for the reception of persons of quality. However, on Sir John's further insistence he put on his clothes, struck a light, descended, and did his utmost to make the nocturnal visitor comfortable, even surrendering to him his own bed, and sending his wife to sleep with the children. Sir John cast himself on the bed. He tossed; and host and hostess heard him cry out, and speak of enemies who pursued him and sought his blood.

There was no sleeping for Daniel or his wife, and the host rose at dawn to join a neighbour in mowing a meadow. But when he was about to go forth, his wife begged not to be left in the house alone with the strange gentleman. The neighbour came up, and he and Alley spoke together at the door. Their voices reached Sir John, who had fallen into a disordered sleep. Persuaded that the enemies were arrived and were surrounding the house, he rushed out in his nightgown, with his sword drawn, fell on his host, and killed him. Then he ran his sword against the wife, wounding her. But now, with the gathering light, he discovered what he had done, and in a fit of despair stabbed himself in two places. He was secured now by neighbours who had come up, and taken to the bed he had just quitted. A surgeon was sent for, and his wounds were bound up. But Sir John angrily refused the assistance of the leech, and tore away the bandages, and bled to death.

Daniel Alley was buried on the 8th day of August, 1605, and Sir John Fitz on the 10th, and "because he was a Gentleman born and of good kindred, he was buried in the Chancel at Twickenham."

Sir 'Judas' Stukeley

Sir Lewis Stukeley, or Stucley, who has been branded as the Judas of Devonshire, was the eldest son of John Stukeley, of Affeton, by Frances St Leger. He had two brothers and several sisters. He was great-nephew to "Lusty" Stucley, and partook of that vein of meanness and treachery that characterized Thomas. He was married to Frances daughter of Anthony Monk, of Potheridge, a family which, if not more ancient, was free from the taint of baseness that savoured three of the Stukeleys. By her he had five sons; none were knighted, the shame of the father rested on them, and it was not till the next generation that knighthood was again granted to the representative of the Stukeleys of Affeton.

Lewis himself was knighted, not for any worthiness that he had shown, but as the representative of a good family, when James I was on his way to London in 1603. In 1617 he was appointed guardian of Thomas Rolfe, the infant son of Pocahontas by John Rolfe. Then he was created Vice-Admiral of Devon, and in that capacity he left London in June, 1618, with verbal orders from the King to arrest Sir Walter Raleigh, then arrived at Plymouth on his return from the Orinoco.

Sir Walter had been released from his long captivity in the Tower, because he gave hopes to James of finding a gold-mine in Guiana. He had been there before, had brought away auriferous spar, and had heard tidings of deposits of gold. James was in debt and in need of money, and he clutched at the chance of getting out of his difficulties through the gold of Guiana. That there was gold there is certain; Raleigh's mine has been identified; but since he had left the Orinoco, the Spaniards had pushed up the river and annexed land and built stations.

James did not want to break with the Spanish Government and gave Raleigh instructions not to come to blows with the

Spaniards. Unhappily, Raleigh's lieutenant, whom he had dispatched up the river, did come to blows with them, and blood was shed; it was however in self-defence, for the Spaniards had fallen upon the English party when unprepared and killed some of them. This unfortunate business, and the fact that Raleigh could not reach his gold-mine, the way to it being intercepted by the Spaniards, made him turn back with a heavy heart. On reaching Plymouth, he hastened towards London to state the case to the King, when he was met at Ashburton by his cousin, Sir Lewis Stukeley, with smiles and professions of love – but having war in his heart. His rancour against his kinsman was due to a quarrel in 1584, when, as Stukeley asserted, Sir Walter did "extreme injustice" to Stukeley's father, then a volunteer in Sir Richard Grenville's Virginia voyage, by deceiving him in a matter of a venture he had made. James was in a great fright lest he should be plunged in war with the King of Spain, and very angry because the gold-mine had not been found; and Stukeley was promised £500 to worm out of his cousin some damning admissions, as that there never had been any goldmine at all, and to betray these to James. Stukeley had received only verbal instructions from the King. He therefore reconducted Raleigh back to Plymouth, where he placed him in Radford, the house of Sir Christopher Harris, who was charged with his custody, till Stukeley received orders from James. Raleigh was ill – or feigned to be ill – the former is the more probable, and he being laxly guarded formed a plan of escape to France. He commissioned Captain King, the only one of his officers who remained faithful to the last, to make arrangements for flight with the master of a French vessel then lying in the Sound. At nightfall, the two stole from Radford and got into a boat lying at the little quay below the house. They had not rowed far, however, before qualms came over Raleigh; it seemed to him unworthy of his past and of his honour to fly his native land; perhaps he counted too securely on the generosity of the despicable James. He changed

45

his mind, and ordered King to return to Radford. Next day he sent money to the Frenchman, and begged him to wait for him another night. Night came, but Raleigh did not stir. This singular irresolution in a man so energetic, ready, and firm, points surely to the fact that he was ill at the time, suffering from the ague which so often prostrated him. Stukeley at length received orders to take his prisoner to London, and the opportunity to escape was gone for ever. As Raleigh passed through Sherborne, he pointed out the lands that had once been his, and related how wrongfully they had been taken from him.

At Salisbury Raleigh complained of illness, and begged to be allowed to halt there for a while. It was asserted by a French quack, Mannourie, set as a spy over him, that he got the doctor to anoint him so as to produce sores wherever the ointment was applied. This was one of the charges afterwards brought against him, at the special insistence of King James, who always kept his eye on trifles. Whilst Raleigh was at Salisbury, Sir Lewis Stukeley robbed him of all his jewels and money, leaving him only the emerald ring on his finger, engraved with the Raleigh arms. It has been asserted that Sir Walter endeavoured here to bribe his cousin to connive at his escape. Had this been the case, Stukeley would certainly have mentioned it in his "Humble Petition" and justification of his conduct after the execution of Raleigh. He was not the man to fail to flaunt such a feather in his cap as that he had resisted a bribe, had such a bribe been offered him.

Whilst Raleigh lay ill at Salisbury, Captain King hurried up to London, by his master's direction, to hire a vessel to wait at Gravesend till he should be able to go on board. The master of the vessel at once betrayed the matter. Sir William St John, a captain of one of the King's ships, immediately took horse and rode to meet Stukeley and his prisoner on their way to town, and encountered them before he reached Bagshot. Stukeley then confided to him certain charges against Raleigh which he was to lay before the King.

Next day Stukeley had fresh matter to dispatch to the Court. It was this: La Chesnée, the interpreter of the French Embassy, visited Sir Walter at Brentford. He had brought with him a message from Le Clerc, agent for the King of France, offering him a passage on board a French vessel, together with letters of introduction which would secure him an honourable reception in Paris. Raleigh thanked him for the offer, but replied that he had already provided for his escape. All this Stukeley learned by applying his ear to the keyhole or by worming the secret out of Raleigh by professions of kindness and desire to assist him to escape.

James at once took alarm. A plot with France was a serious matter at that time. He accordingly directed Stukeley to continue to counterfeit friendship with Raleigh, to assist him in his meditated escape, and only to arrest him at the last moment; and to bring this attempt as one more charge against Raleigh.

So Stukeley continued to insinuate himself into the confidence of his cousin, and endeavoured, by all means in his power, to wheedle out of him such papers as might afford evidence of his designs and might serve to help to bring him to the scaffold.

On his arrival in town, Raleigh was conducted to his own house in Broad Street. There he was revisited by Le Clerc, who repeated his former offers.

The next morning Sir Walter got into a boat attended by Stukeley, all smiles, and the honest King; and, as prearranged, he was arrested at Woolwich and at once lodged in the Tower.

On 29 October, 1618, Raleigh's head fell under the executioner's axe. He was a victim to Spanish resentment and to James's meanness in offering him as a sacrifice to curry favour with Spain. Gardiner says Raleigh was executed "nominally in accordance with the sentence delivered in 1603; in reality because he had failed to secure the gold of which James was in need. The real crime was the King's, who had sent him out without first defining the limits of Spanish sovereignty."

The writer of the notice of Sir Lewis Stukeley in the *Dictionary of National Biography* takes a lenient view of Stukeley's conduct. "Stukeley certainly gave hostile, not necessarily false evidence against Raleigh. He seems to have been a harsh, narrow-minded and vulgar man, glad to have his cousin in his power, to revenge himself on him for the pecuniary loss his own father had entertained."

Gardiner says: "Stukeley seems to have thought it no shame to act as a spy upon the man who had called upon him to betray his trust;" but it is precisely this charge that cannot be established. We have no good evidence that Raleigh did attempt to bribe him. Popular opinion ran strongly against Stukeley, and he was nicknamed Sir Judas. He tried to hold up his head at Court, but no man would condescend to speak to him. He met on all sides with glances full of contempt and gestures of disgust. He hurried to James, and offered to take the Sacrament upon the truth of a story Raleigh had denied on the scaffold – that he had been offered a commission by the French King (the story came through Mannourie); but no one would have believed Stukeley a whit the readier had he done this.

Indeed, Mannourie subsequently admitted that it was false, when he was arrested for clipping the gold, the blood money, he had received for spying on Sir Walter. In a letter from the Rev T Lorkin to Sir T Puckering on 16 February, 1619, he says: "Mannourie, the French Apothecary, (who joined with Stukeley in the accusation of Sir Walter Raleigh) is at Plymouth for clipping of gold . . . his examination was sent up hither to the King, wherein . . . (as I hear from Sir Rob. Winde, cupbearer I think to his Majesty, who saith he read the examination) that his accusation against Raleigh was false, and that he was won thereto by the practise and importunity of Stukeley, and now acknowledges this his present miserable condition a judgment of God upon him for that."

When Stukeley made this offer to King James, a bystander

dryly observed that if the King would order him to be beheaded, and if he would then confirm the truth of his story with an oath while on the scaffold, then possibly he might be believed.

One day Sir Judas went to call on the old Earl of Nottingham, who was Lord High Admiral, and asked to be allowed to speak to him. The Earl turned on him instantly. "What," he said, "thou base fellow! Thou who art reputed the scorn and contempt of men, how darest thou offer thyself into my presence? Were it not in my own house, I would cudgel thee with my staff for presuming to be so saucy." Stukeley ran off to whine to the King, but even there he met with no redress. "What," said James, "wouldst thou have me do? Wouldst thou have me hang him? On my soul, if I should hang all that speak ill of thee, all the trees in the country would not suffice." It was even said, probably without truth, that James had said to Stukeley, "Sir Walter's blood be on thy head."

A few days after the scene with the King, it was discovered that Stukeley had been for many years engaged in the nefarious occupation of clipping coin. It was even said that he tampered in this way with the very gold pieces which had been paid to him as the price of his services for lodging Raleigh in the Tower and betraying him. When arrested he endeavoured to excuse himself by inculpating his son. Could meanness descend to a lower depth?

"1619 Jan. 12. Upon Twelfth Night Stukeley was committed close prisoner in the Gate house for clipping of gold. He had received of the Exchequer some weeks before £500 in recompense for the service he had performed in the business of Sir Walter Raleigh, and began (as is said) to exercise the trade upon that ill-gotten money (the price of blood).

"Upon examination he endeavoured to avoid it from himself, by casting the burden either upon his son or man. The former plays least in sight and can not be found. The servant is committed to the Marshalsey, who, understanding that his Master would shift over the business to him, is willing to set the saddle upon the right horse, and accuses his Master."

But the accusation was not pressed. King James owed Stukeley too deep a debt to let him suffer, and he threw him a pardon, so that the evidence against him was not gone into. It may be remembered that "Lusty" Stukeley had also been implicated in clipping and coining, and had only escaped arrest by flying the country.

Stukeley, an outcast from society in London, went down to Affeton. But even there he was ill-received. The gentry would not speak to him, his own retainers viewed him with a cold, if not hostile, eye, and rendered him but bare obedience.

The brand of Cain was on him, and he fled from the society of his fellow men to the Isle of Lundy, and shut himself up in the lonely, haunted tower of the De Mariscoes. There he went raving mad and perished (1620), a miserable lunatic on that rock, surrounded by the roaring of the waves and the shrieks of the wind. His body was conveyed to South Molton, so that he was denied even a grave beside his ancestors at Affeton.

Jack Rattenbury

The coasts of Devon and Cornwall, north and south, are bold, with cliffs starting out of the sea, white near the Dorset frontier, then red, and then of limestone marble, or, on the north coast, of slate and schist. The rocks are riddled with caves, the highland is cleft by narrow valleys sawn through their mass by descending streams. The whole coast, north and south, lends itself to smuggling; and smuggling had been carried on as a profitable speculation till it ceased to pay, when heavy duties were removed, and when the coastguard became efficient.

The smugglers formerly ran their goods into the caves when the weather permitted, or the preventive men were not on the look-out. They stowed away their goods in the caves, and gave notice to the farmers and gentry of the neighbourhood, all of whom were provided with numerous donkeys, which were forthwith sent down to the caches, and the kegs and bales were removed under cover of night or of storm. Few farmhouses and squires' mansions were not also provided with hiding-places in which to store the kegs obtained from the free-traders. Only the week before writing this I was shown one such in the depth of a dense wood, at Sandridge Park on the Dart; externally it would have been taken for a natural mound or a tumulus. But there are a concealed door and a descent by a flight of steps into the subterranean cellar, that was carefully vaulted and carefully drained.

A very noticeable feature of the Devon and Cornwall coasts is the trenched and banked-up paths from the little coves. By these paths the kegs and bales were removed under cover of night.

As an excuse for keeping droves of donkeys, it was pretended that the sea-sand and the kelp served as admirable dressing for the land; and no doubt so they did; the trains of asses sometimes came up laden with sacks of sand, but not infrequently with kegs of brandy.

Now a wary preventive man might watch too narrowly the proceedings of these trains of asses. Accordingly squires, yeomen and farmers alike set to work to cut deep ways in the face of the downs, along the slopes of the hills, and bank them up, so that whole caravans of laden beasts might travel up and down absolutely unseen from the sea and greatly screened from the land side.

Undoubtedly the sunken ways and the high banks are a great protection against the weather. So they were represented to be – and no doubt greatly were the good folks commended for their consideration for the beasts and their drivers, in thus at great cost shutting them off from the violence of the gale. Nevertheless, it can hardly be doubted that concealment from the eye of the coastguard was sought by this means quite as much as, if not more than, the sheltering the beasts of burden from the weather.

A few years ago, an old church-house in my own parish was demolished. The church-house was originally the place where the parishioners from a distance, in a country district, put up between the morning and afternoon services on the Sunday, and was used for "church ales", etc. It was always a long building of two stories; that below served for the men, that above for the women, and each had its great fireplace. Here they ate and chattered between services, as already said, and here were served with ale by the sexton or clerk. In a great many cases these church-houses have been converted into taverns. Now this one in the writer's parish had never been thus altered. When it was pulled down, it was found that the floor of large slate slabs in the lower room was undermined with hollows like graves, only of much larger dimensions – and these had served for the concealment of smuggled spirits. The clerk had, in fact, dug them out, and did a little trade on Sundays with selling contraband liquor from these stores.

The story is told of a certain baronet near Dartmouth, now

deceased, who had a handsome house and park near the coast. The preventive men had long suspected that Sir Thomas had done more than wink at the proceedings of the receivers of smuggled goods. His park dipped in graceful undulations to the sea and to a lovely creek, in which was his boathouse. But they never had been able to establish the fact that he favoured the smugglers, and allowed them to use his grounds and outbuildings.

However, at last, one night a party of men with kegs on their shoulders were seen stealing through the park towards the mansion. They were observed also leaving without the kegs. Accordingly, next morning the officer in command called, together with several underlings. He apologized to the baronet for any inconvenience his visit might occasion – he was quite sure that Sir Thomas was ignorant of the use made of his park, his landing-place, even of his house – but there was evidence that "run" goods had been brought to the mansion the preceding night, and it was but the duty of the officer to point this out to Sir Thomas, and ask him to permit a search – which would be conducted with all the delicacy possible.

The baronet, an exceedingly urbane man, promptly expressed his readiness to allow house, cellar, attic – every part of his house, and every outbuilding – unreservedly to be searched. He produced his keys. The cellar was, of course, the place where wine and spirits were most likely to be found – let that be explored first. He had a cellar-book, which he produced, and he would be glad if the officer would compare what he found below with his entries in the book. The search was made with some zest, for the Government officers had long looked on Sir Thomas with mistrust; and yet were somewhat disarmed by the frankness with which he met them.

They ransacked the mansion from garret to cellar, and every part of the outbuildings, and found nothing. They had omitted to look into the family coach, which was full of rum kegs, so full that, to prevent the springs being broken or showing that the carriage was laden, the axle-trees were "trigged up" below with blocks of wood.

When a train of asses or mules conveyed contraband goods along a road, it was often customary to put stockings over the hoofs to deaden the sound of their steps.

The principal ports to which the smugglers ran were Cherbourg and Roscoff; but also to the Channel Islands. During the European War, and when Napoleon had formed, and forced on the humbled nations of Europe, his great scheme for the exclusion of English goods from all ports, our smugglers did a rare business in conveying prohibited English wares to France and returning with smuggled spirits to our shores, reaping a harvest both ways. If a revenue cutter hove in sight and gave chase, they sank their kegs, but with a small buoy above to indicate where they were, and afterwards they would return and "creep" for them with grappling irons. But the preventive officers were on the alert, and although they might find no contraband on the vessel they overhauled, yet the officers threw out their irons and searched the sea in the wake of the ship, and kept a sharp look-out for the buoys. If the contraband articles were brought ashore, and there was no opportunity to remove them at once, they were buried in the sand, to be exhumed when the coast was clear.

The smugglers had more enemies to contend with than the preventive men. As they were known to be daring and experienced sailors, they were in great request to man the navy, and every crib and den was searched for them that they might be impressed.

The life was hard, full of risks, and although these men sometimes made great hauls, yet they as often lost their cargoes and their vessels. They were very frequently in the pay of merchants in England, who provided them with their ships and bailed them out when they were arrested. Rarely did a smuggler realize a competence, he almost invariably ended his days in poverty. One of the most notorious of the Devon free-traders was Jack Rattenbury, who was commonly called "the Rob-Roy of the West". He wrote his *Memoirs* when advanced in life, and when he had given up smuggling, not that the trade had lost its attraction for him, but because he suffered from gout, and he ended his days as a contractor for blue-lias lime for the harbour in course of erection at Sidmouth.

It will not be necessary to give the life of this man in full. It was divided into two periods – his career on a privateer and his career as a smuggler – spent partly in fishing, partly as a pilot, mainly in carrying on free trade in spirits, between Cherbourg, or the Channel Islands, and Devon. Naturally, Rattenbury speaks of himself and his comrades as all honourable men, it is the informers who are the spawn of hell. The record year by year of his exploits as a smuggler, presents little variety, and the same may be said of his deeds as a privateer. We shall therefore give but a few instances of his career in both epochs of his life.

John Rattenbury was born at Beer in the year 1778. Beer lies in a cleft of the chalk hills, and consists of one long street of cottages from the small harbour. His father was a shoemaker, but tired of his awl and leather apron, he cast both aside and went on board a man-of-war before John was born, and was never heard of more. It is possible that Mrs Rattenbury's tongue may have been the stimulating cause of his desertion of the last.

The mother of John, frugal and industrious, sold fish for her support and that of her child, and contrived to maintain herself and him without seeking parish relief.

The boy naturally took to the water, as all the men of Beer were fishermen or smugglers, and at the age of nine he went in the boat with his uncle after fish, but happening one day when left in charge to lose the rudder of the row-boat, his uncle gave him the rope's end so severely that the boy ran away and went as apprentice to a Brixham fisherman; but this man also beat and otherwise maltreated him, and again he ran away.

As he could get no employment at Beer, he went to Bridport and engaged on board a vessel in the coasting trade. But he did not remain long with his master and returned to Beer, where he found his uncle entering men for privateering, and this fired John Rattenbury's ambition and he volunteered.

"About the latter end of March, 1792, we proceeded on our first cruise off the Western Islands: and even now, notwithstanding the lapse of years, I can recall the triumph and exultation which rushed through my veins as I saw the shores of my native land recede, and the vast ocean opening before me."

Instead of making prizes, the privateer and her crew were made a prize of and conveyed to Bordeaux, where the crew were detained as prisoners. John Rattenbury, however, contrived to make his escape to an American vessel lying in the harbour, on which, after detention for twelve months, he sailed to New York. There he entered on an American vessel bound for Copenhagen, and on reaching that place invested all the money he had earned and carried away with him from Bordeaux in fiddles and clothes. Then he sailed in another American vessel for Guernsey, where he profitably disposed of his fiddles and clothes. He had engaged with the captain for the whole voyage to New York, but when at Guernsey at his request the captain allowed him to return to England to visit his family, on passing his word that he would rejoin the ship within a specified time. Rattenbury returned to Beer, and broke his promise, which he regards as a mistake. He remained at home six months occupied in fishing, "but," says he, "I found the employment very dull and tiresome after the roving life I had led; and as the smuggling trade was then plied very briskly in the neighbourhood, I determined to try my fortune in it." Fortune in smuggling as in gambling favours beginners so as to lure them on. However, after a few months, Rattenbury had lapses into the paths of honesty.

In one of these, soon after, he did one of the most brilliant achievements of his life. I will give it in his own words:

"Being in want of a situation, I applied to Captain Jarvis, and agreed to go with him in a vessel called the *Friends,* which belonged to Beer and Seaton. As soon as she was rigged we proceeded to sea, but, contrary winds coming on, we were obliged to put into Lyme; the next day, the wind being favourable, we put to sea again, and proceeded to Tenby, where we were bound for culm [anthracite slack, used in lime-kilns].

"At eight o'clock the captain set the watch, and it was my turn to remain below; at twelve I went on deck and counted till four, when I went below again, but was scarcely dropped asleep, when I was aroused by hearing the captain exclaim, 'Come on deck, my good fellow! Here is a privateer, and we shall all be taken.' When I got up, I found the privateer close alongside of us. The captain hailed us in English, and asked us from what port we came and where we were bound. Our captain told the exact truth, and he then sent a boat with an officer in her to take all hands on board his own vessel, which he did, except myself and a little boy, who had never been to sea before. He then sent the prize-master and four men on board our brig, with orders to take her into the nearest French port. When the privateer was gone, the prize-master ordered me to go aloft and loose the main top-gallant sail.

"When I came down, I perceived that he was steering very wildly through ignorance of the coast, and I offered to take the helm, to which he consented, and directed me to steer south-east by south. He went below, and was engaged in drinking and carousing with his companions. They likewise sent me up a glass of grog occasionally which animated my spirits, and I began to conceive a hope not only of escaping, but also of being revenged on the enemy. A fog too came on, which befriended the design I had in view; I therefore altered the course to east by north, expecting that we might fall in with some English vessel.

"As the day advanced the fog gradually dispersed, and, the sky getting clearer, we could perceive land; the prize-master and his companions asked me what land it was; I told them that it was Alderney, which they believed, though at the same time we were just off Portland. We then hauled our wind more to the south until we cleared the Bill; soon after we came in sight of land off St Alban's: the prize-master then again asked what land it was which we saw; I told him it was Cape La Hogue.

"My companions then became suspicious and angry, thinking I had deceived them, and they took a dog that had belonged to our captain, and threw him overboard in a great rage and knocked down his house. This was done as a caution to intimate to me what would be my fate if I had deceived them. We were now within a league of Swanage, and I persuaded them to go on shore to get a pilot: they then hoisted out a boat, into which I got with three of them, not without serious apprehension as to what would be the event.

"We now came so near the shore that the people hailed us, and told them to keep further west. My companions began to swear, and said the people spoke English: this I denied, and urged them to hail again; but as they were rising to do so, I plunged overboard and came up the other side of the boat; they then struck at me with their oars, and snapped a pistol at me, but it missed fire. I still continued swimming, and every time they attempted to strike me, I made a dive and disappeared. The boat in which they were now took water, and finding they were engaged in a vain pursuit, and endangering their own safety, they suddenly turned round, and rowed away as fast as possible to regain the vessel. Having got rid of my foes, I put forth all my efforts to get to the shore, which I at last accomplished.

"In the meantime, the men in the boat reached the brig, and spreading all canvas, bore away for the French coast. Being afraid they would get off with the vessel, I immediately sent one man to the signal-house at St Alban's and another to Swanage, to obtain all the assistance they could to bring her back.

"Fortunately, there was at the time in Swanage Bay a small cutter, belonging to His Majesty's Customs, called the *Nancy*, commanded by Captain Willis; and as soon as he had received the information, he made all sail after them; but I was not on board, not being able to reach them in time. The cutter came up with the brig, and by retaking, brought her into Cowes the same night, where the men were put in prison. Captain Willis then sent me a letter, stating what he had done, and advising me to go as quickly as possible to the owners, and inform them of all that had taken place. This I did without delay, and one of them immediately set off for Cowes, when he got her back by paying salvage – but I never received any reward for the service I had rendered, either from the owners or from any other quarter."

John Rattenbury was then aged sixteen.

As Rattenbury was returning to Devon in a cutter, the vessel was stopped and overhauled by a lieutenant and his gang seeking able-bodied seamen to impress them. "When it came to my turn to be examined, I told him I was an apprentice, and that my name was German Phillips (that being the name of a young man whose indenture I had for a protection). This stratagem was of no avail with the keen-eyed lieutenant, and he took me immediately on board the *Royal William*, a guard ship, then lying at Spithead. I remained in close confinement for a month, hoping by some chance I might be able to effect my escape; but seeing no prospect of accomplishing my design, I at last volunteered my services for the Royal Navy; if that can be called a voluntary act, which is the effect of necessity, not of inclination.

"And here I cannot help making a remark on the common practice of impressing seamen in time of war. Our country is called the land of liberty; we possess a just and invincible aversion to slavery at home and in our foreign colonies, and it is triumphantly said that a slave cannot breathe in England. Yet how is this to be reconciled with the practice of tearing men from their weeping and afflicted families, and from the peaceable and useful pursuits of merchandise and commerce, and chaining them to a situation which is alike repugnant to their feelings and their principles?"

At Spithead Rattenbury succeeded in making his escape. But he had left his pocket-book on board, and by this means the lieutenant found out what were his real name and abode, and thenceforth he was hunted as a deserter and put to great shifts to save himself from capture.

In 1800, when he was twenty-one, he was taken in a vessel by a Spanish privateer and brought to Vigo; but on shore made himself so useful and was so cheerful that he was given his liberty and travelled on foot to Oporto, where he found a vessel bound for Guernsey, laden with oranges and lemons, and worked his way home in her.

"Before I set out on my last voyage, I had fixed my affections on a young woman in the neighbourhood, and we were married on the 17th of April, 1801. We then went to reside at Lyme, and finding that I could not obtain regular employment at home, I again determined to try my fortune in privateering, and accordingly engaged myself with Captain Diamond of the *Alert*."

But this expedition led to no results. No captures were made; Rattenbury returned home as poor as when he started, and almost at once acted as pilot to foreign vessels. On one occasion a lieutenant came on board to impress men, and took Rattenbury and put him in confinement. Next day he told the lieutenant that if he would accompany him to Lyme, he would show him a public-house where he was sure to find men he could impress. The officer consented and landed with Jack and some other seamen, and proceeded to the tavern; but finding none there he ordered Rattenbury back to the boat.

At that moment up came Rattenbury's wife, and he made a rush to escape whilst she threw herself upon the lieutenant and had a scuffle with him; and as the townsfolk took her part, Rattenbury escaped.

On another occasion he was at Weymouth, and the same lieutenant, learning this fact, tracked him to the tavern where he slept, and burst in at 2 am. Rattenbury had just time to climb up the chimney before the officer and his men entered. They searched the house, but could not find him. When they were gone he descended bruised, half-stifled, and covered with soot.

"Wearied out by the incessant pursuit of my enemies, and finding that I was followed by them from place to place like a hunted stag by the hounds, I at last determined, with a view to getting rid of them, again to go privateering." Accordingly he shipped on board the *Unity* cutter and cruised about Madeira and Teneriffe, looking out for prizes. But this expedition was as unsuccessful as the other, and in August, 1805, "I determined never again to engage in privateering, a resolution which I have ever since kept, and of which I have never repented."

"On my return home, I engaged ostensibly in the trade of fishing, but in reality was principally employed in that of smuggling. My first voyage was to Christchurch, in an open boat, where we took in a cargo of contraband goods, and, on our return, safely landed the whole.

"Being elated with this success, we immediately proceeded to the same port again, but on our way we fell in with the *Roebuck* tender: a warm chase ensued; and, in firing at us, a man named Slaughter, on board the tender, had the misfortune to blow his arm off. Eventually, the enemy came up with and captured us; and, on being taken on board, found the captain in a great rage in consequence of the accident and he swore he would put us all on board a man-of-war. He got his boat out to take the wounded man on shore; and, while this was going forward, I watched an opportunity, and stowed myself away in her, unknown to any person there. I remained without being perceived, amidst the confusion that prevailed; and when they reached the shore, I left the boat, and got clear off.

"The same night, I went in a boat that I had borrowed, along-

61

side the tender, and rescued all my companions; we likewise brought three kegs of gin away with us, and landed safe at Weymouth, from whence we made the best of our way home.

"The same winter I made seven voyages in a smuggling vessel which had just been built; five of them were attended with success, and two of them turned out failures.

"In the spring of 1806, I went to Alderney, where we took in a cargo; but, returning, fell in with the *Duke of York* cutter, in consequence of getting too near her boat in a fog without perceiving her. Being unable to make our escape, we were immediately put on board the cutter, and the crew picked up some of our kegs which were floating near by, but we had previously sunk the principal part.

"As soon as we were secured, the captain called us into his cabin, and told us that if we would take up the kegs for him, he would give us our boat and liberty, on the honour of a gentleman. To this proposal we agreed, and having pointed out where they lay, we took them up for him. We then expected that the captain would have been as good as his word; but, instead of doing so, he disgracefully departed from it, and a fresh breeze springing up, we steered away hard for Dartmouth. When we came alongside the castle, the cutter being then going at the rate of six knots, I jumped overboard; but having a boat in her stern, they immediately lowered her with a man. I succeeded, however, in getting on shore, and concealed myself among some bushes; but two women who saw me go into the thicket inadvertently told the boat's crew where I was, upon which they retook me, and I was carried on board quite exhausted with the fatigue and loss of blood, for I had cut myself in different places."

Next morning Rattenbury was brought up before the magistrates at Dartmouth along with his comrades in misfortune, and they were sentenced to pay a fine of a hundred pounds each, or else to serve on board a man-of-war, or go to prison.

They elected the last, and were confined in a wretched den

where they could hardly move and breathe. Worn out by their discomfort, they agreed to enlist, and were liberated and removed to a brig in Dartmouth roads. On coming on board he found all the officers drinking; the mainsail had been partly hoisted, so that the officers could not command a prospect of the shore. Seizing his opportunity he jumped overboard, and seeing a boat approaching held up his hand to the man in it, as a signal to be taken up. The fellow did so, and in less than five minutes he was landed at Kingswear opposite Dartmouth. He paid the fisherman a pound, and made his way to Brixham, where he hired a fishing-smack and got safely home.

Soon after, he purchased part of a galley, and resumed his smuggling expeditions, and made several successful trips in her, till he lost his galley at sea. Then he went to Alderney in an open boat, with two other men, to get kegs, but on their way back were chased, captured, and carried into Falmouth, where he was sentenced to be sent to gaol at Bodmin.

"We were put into two post-chaises, with two constables to take care of us. As our guards stopped at almost every public-house, towards evening they became pretty merry. When we came to the Indian Queen – a public-house a few miles from Bodmin – while the constables were taking their potations, I bribed the drivers not to interfere. Having finished, the constables ordered us again into the chaise, but we refused. A scuffle ensued. One of them collared me, some blows were exchanged, and he fired a pistol, the ball of which went close to my head. My companion in the meantime was encountering the other constable, and he called on the drivers to assist, but they said it was their duty to attend the horses. We soon got the upper hand of our opponents, and seeing a cottage near, I ran towards it, and the woman who occupied it was so kind as to show me through her house into the garden and to point out the road."

Eventually he reached Newquay with his comrade. Thence they hired horses to Mevagissey, where they took a boat for

Budleigh Salterton. On the following day they walked to Beer.

This is but a sample of one year out of many. He was usually engaged in shady operations, getting him into trouble. On one occasion he undertook to carry four French officers across the Channel who had made their escape from the prison at Tiverton, for the sum of a hundred pounds, but was caught, and narrowly escaped severe punishment.

Soon after that he was arrested as a deserter, by a lieutenant of the sea-fencibles when he was in a public-house drinking along with a sergeant and some privates. But he broke away and jumped into the cellar, where he divested himself of shirt and jacket, armed himself with a reaping-hook, and closing the lower part of a half-hatch door stood at bay, vowing he would reap down the first man who ventured to attack him. His appearance was so formidable, his resolution was so well known, that the soldiers, ten in number, hesitated. As they stood doubtful as to what to do, some women ran into the house crying out that a vessel had drifted ashore, and a boy was in danger of being drowned, that help was urgently needed. This attracted the attention of the soldiers, and whilst they were discussing what was to be done, Rattenbury leaped over the hatch, dashed through the midst of them, and being without jacket and shirt slipped between their fingers. He ran to the beach, jumped into a boat, got on board his vessel, and hoisted the colours. The story told by the women was a device to distract the attention of his assailants. The lieutenant was furious, especially at seeing the colours flying, as a sign of triumph on the part of Rattenbury, who spread sail and scudded away to Alderney, took in a cargo of contraband spirits, and returned safely with it.

We need not follow him through a succession of hairsbreadth escapes, of successes and losses, imprisonments and frauds. He carries on his story to 1836, when, so little had he profited by his free-trading expeditions, that he was fain to accept a pension from Lord Rolle of a shilling a week.